Making History: The Obamas

Barack Obama
Man of Destiny

Amelie von Zumbusch

PowerKids press
New York

Published in 2010 by The Rosen Publishing Group, Inc.
29 East 21st Street, New York, NY 10010

Copyright © 2010 by The Rosen Publishing Group, Inc.

All rights reserved. No part of this book may be reproduced in any form without permission in writing from the publisher, except by a reviewer.

First Edition

Editors: Nicole Pristash and Maggie Murphy
Book Design: Kate Laczynski
Layout Design: Greg Tucker
Photo Researcher: Jessica Gerweck

Photo Credits: Cover Jewel Samad/AFP/Getty Images; p. 4 Sara D. Davis/Getty Images; pp. 6, 8, 10 © Rapport/Newscom; pp. 6 (inset), 16 © Associated Press/AP Images; p. 12 Peter Vanderwarker/Getty Images; p. 12 (inset) Steve Liss/Time & Life Pictures/Getty Images; p. 14 Pascal Le Segretain/Getty Images; p. 18 Jeff Swensen/Getty Images; p. 20 Saul Loeb/AFP/Getty Images.

Library of Congress Cataloging-in-Publication Data

Zumbusch, Amelie von.
 Barack Obama : man of destiny / Amelie von Zumbusch.
     p. cm. — (Making history: The Obamas)
 Includes bibliographical references and index.
 ISBN 978-1-4358-9387-0 (library binding) — ISBN 978-1-4358-9866-0 (pbk.) — ISBN 978-1-4358-9867-7 (6-pack)
 1. Obama, Barack—Juvenile literature. 2. Presidents—United States—Biography—Juvenile literature. 3. Racially mixed people—United States–Biography—Juvenile literature. I. Title.
 E908.Z86 2010
 973.932092—dc22
 [B]
                                             2009033097

Manufactured in the United States of America

CPSIA Compliance Information: Batch #WW10PK: For Further Information contact Rosen Publishing, New York, New York at 1-800-237-9932

Contents

An Inspiring Story 5
A Child of the World 7
Learning About Life 9
Discovering His Roots 11
Law School 13
Meeting Michelle 15
A Home in Chicago 17
Yes We Can 19
A Busy Life 21
New Challenges 22
Glossary 23
Index 24
Web Sites 24

An Inspiring Story

Barack Obama is an **inspiration** to many people. He is the first African American to become president of the United States. Obama's story proves that any child from any background can become the president.

When Obama ran for president in 2008, many people said that he was too young and too unknown to win. Some people claimed that the American people were not ready to pick an African American as their leader. However, Obama believed in both himself and the American people. Obama's hopeful plans for change in America inspired voters. He won the presidential election on November 4, 2008.

As president, Obama often gives speeches about important issues. Here, he is shown speaking to a crowd about health care in Raleigh, North Carolina.

A Child of the World

Obama's parents met while they were students at the University of Hawaii. Obama's mother, Ann Dunham, was born in Kansas. His father, also named Barack Obama, came from Kenya. The pair came from very different worlds, and they were interested in each other's lives. In time, Obama's parents fell in love and got married. On August 4, 1961, young Barack was born.

Sadly, Barack's parents **divorced** when he was a young child. At first, Barack lived with his mother and grandparents in Hawaii. Later, Barack and his mother, who had gotten remarried, moved to Indonesia. This is where Barack's half sister Maya was born.

Here, young Obama sits with his step father, Lolo Soetoro (left), mother (back center), and half sister (front center). *Inset:* Barack Obama Sr.

Learning About Life

Obama's mother wanted him to get the best education possible. In 1971, she sent him to the Punahou School, in Honolulu, Hawaii. As someone with a white mother and a black father, Barack had to figure out how he fit in with the other kids there. Obama continued to search for his **identity** as a student at Occidental College, in California, and Columbia University, in New York.

After finishing his studies at Columbia in 1983, Obama took a job in New York. However, he felt that he should be doing more to help others. Obama moved to Chicago in 1985 to work with people in poor neighborhoods.

When Obama was studying at Columbia University, his grandparents visited him. They were very proud of his accomplishments.

Discovering His Roots

Growing up, Obama saw little of his father. Barack Obama Sr. moved back to Kenya when his son was young, and he visited young Barack only once. Barack Sr. died in 1982 before his son really got a chance to know him. Obama did not know his Kenyan family either. While he was living in Chicago, one of Obama's half siblings from Kenya, Auma, visited him. She suggested that Barack go to Kenya.

Obama visited his father's family in Kenya in 1988. He met many family members there. He also started feeling at peace with his identity and his place in the world.

In Kenya, Barack Obama spent time with the woman who raised his father, shown here. Although they are not related, he calls her his grandmother.

Law School

In the fall of 1988, Obama started his studies at Harvard Law School, in Cambridge, Massachusetts. Obama had made a difference while working in Chicago's poor neighborhoods. However, he felt that he could help more people if he became a **lawyer**. That way, he could work to change laws and make sure everyone had a fair chance.

At Harvard, Obama became the first African-American president of the *Harvard Law Review*, a law journal. This was a big honor for him. As president of the *Review*, Obama got the chance to work with all types of people. He became good at getting people to work together.

Harvard Law School, shown here, is one of the best law schools. *Inset:* Obama after being elected president of the *Harvard Law Review*.

Meeting Michelle

While he was in law school, Obama worked for a law firm in Chicago during the summer. There, a young lawyer named Michelle Robinson was picked to mentor, or teach and guide, him. Obama thought Michelle was smart and beautiful. Soon, the two started dating.

After law school, Obama took time off to write a book about his struggle to find his identity. The book, *Dreams from My Father*, was well received. It went on to become a best seller. After finishing his book, Obama moved to Chicago to become a lawyer. In 1992, he married Michelle Robinson.

When Barack Obama became president, his wife, Michelle (left), became the First Lady of the United States.

A Home in Chicago

The Obamas settled in Chicago. In time, they had two daughters, Malia and Sasha. Obama cared deeply about Chicago, and he worked to make it a better place. He worked as a lawyer and taught law. Obama also served in the Illinois state **senate**.

By 2003, Obama felt that he could make a bigger difference as a U.S. senator in Washington. He was elected to the U.S. Senate in 2004. There, Obama helped make a law that lets people track how the government spends money. He also looked out for **veterans**, and he tried to keep America's enemies from getting powerful **weapons**.

As a U.S. senator, Obama listened to people's concerns. Here, he meets with workers who became sick at their jobs at an Illinois weapons factory.

Yes We Can

Although he accomplished much as a U.S. senator, Obama thought about a higher job. In February 2007, he said that he would run for president.

Many people doubted that Obama could win because he was not well known. However, Obama believed that America was ready for change. Obama's **slogan** was "Yes We Can." He believed that America could become a better country, and he wanted **Democrats** and **Republicans** to work together. First, Obama won over voters in **primary** elections. Then, he became the Democrats' **candidate**. Finally, Obama went on to win the presidential election against the Republican candidate, Senator John McCain.

Days before Ohio's Democratic primary election on March 4, 2008, Obama spoke to supporters about the changes he would make as president.

A Busy Life

On January 20, 2009, Barack Obama became the forty-fourth president of the United States. Millions of people traveled to Washington, D.C., to see him go from being Senator Obama to President Obama.

Since becoming president, Obama has been very busy. He travels around the world to talk about important things, such as the **environment**, with leaders of other countries. He has worked with U.S. lawmakers to make new jobs and help homeowners in hard times. Obama does not have a lot of free time. When he does have time, though, he likes playing basketball, reading, and spending time with his daughters.

President Obama sometimes travels to other countries. Here, Obama and his family are shown visiting Ghana, in West Africa.

New Challenges

On his first day as president, Obama said that "the **challenges** we face are real, they are serious, and they are many." However, he promised that "they will be met." As all presidents do, Obama will push for the changes he believes will make the United States a better country for everyone.

Though he still has much work ahead of him, Obama has already accomplished more than most people believed he could. In October 2009, Obama won the Nobel Peace Prize. This great honor is given once a year to someone who works to advance world peace. Obama's story gives hope to people around the world.

Glossary

candidate (KAN-dih-dayt) A person who runs in an election.

challenges (CHA-lenj-ez) Things that are hard to deal with.

Democrats (DEH-muh-krats) People who belong to the Democratic Party, one of the two major political parties in the United States.

divorced (dih-VORSD) Ended a marriage legally.

environment (en-VY-ern-ment) All the living things and conditions of a place.

identity (eye-DEN-tuh-tee) Who a person is.

inspiration (in-spuh-RAY-shun) Powerful, moving guidance.

lawyer (LAH-yer) A person who gives advice about the law and who speaks for people in court.

primary (PRY-mer-ee) An election held to pick a candidate for a later election.

Republicans (rih-PUH-blih-kenz) People who belong to the Republican Party, one of the two major political parties in the United States.

senate (SEH-nit) A law-making part of the U.S. government or a state government.

slogan (SLOH-gin) A word or phrase used in politics to sell an idea or a goal.

veterans (VEH-tuh-runz) People who have fought in a war.

weapons (WEH-punz) Objects used to hurt or kill.

Index

A
America, 5, 17, 19. *See also* United States

B
background, 5, 22

C
change(s), 5, 13, 19, 22

E
election(s), 5, 19
environment, 21

I
identity, 9, 11, 15

Illinois state senate, 17
inspiration, 5

L
lawyer, 13, 15, 17
leader(s), 5, 21

P
parents, 7
plans, 5
president(s), 5, 13 19, 21–22

R
Republicans, 19

S
slogan, 19
story, 5, 22
students, 7

U
United States, 5, 21–22. *See also* America
University of Hawaii, 7

V
veterans, 17
voters, 5, 19

W
weapons, 17

Web Sites

Due to the changing nature of Internet links, PowerKids Press has developed an online list of Web sites related to the subject of this book. This site is updated regularly. Please use this link to access the list: www.powerkidslinks.com/obamas/barack/

OCT 27 2010
2/25